AIR MINISTRY.

Directorate of Research.
Kingsway, W.C. 2.

JUNKER (J.I.)

I.C. 671

REPORT

ON THE

JUNKER (ALL-METAL) ARMOURED BIPLANE, TYPE J.I.

JULY, 1919.

H. R. BROOKE-POPHAM,
Brigadier-General,
Director of Research.

The Naval & Military Press Ltd

Published by
The Naval & Military Press Ltd
5 Riverside, Brambleside, Bellbrook
Industrial Estate, Uckfield, East Sussex,
TN22 1QQ England

Tel: +44 (0) 1825 749494
Fax: +44 (0) 1825 765701

www.naval-military-press.com
www.military-genealogy.com

*In reprinting in facsimile from the original, any imperfections are inevitably reproduced
and the quality may fall short of modern type and cartographic standards.*

AIR MINISTRY.

Directorate of Research.

Kingsway, W.C. 2.

JUNKER (J.I.)

I.C. 671

REPORT

ON THE

JUNKER (ALL-METAL) ARMOURED BIPLANE, TYPE J.I.

JULY, 1919.

H. R. BROOKE-POPHAM,
Brigadier-General,
Director of Research.

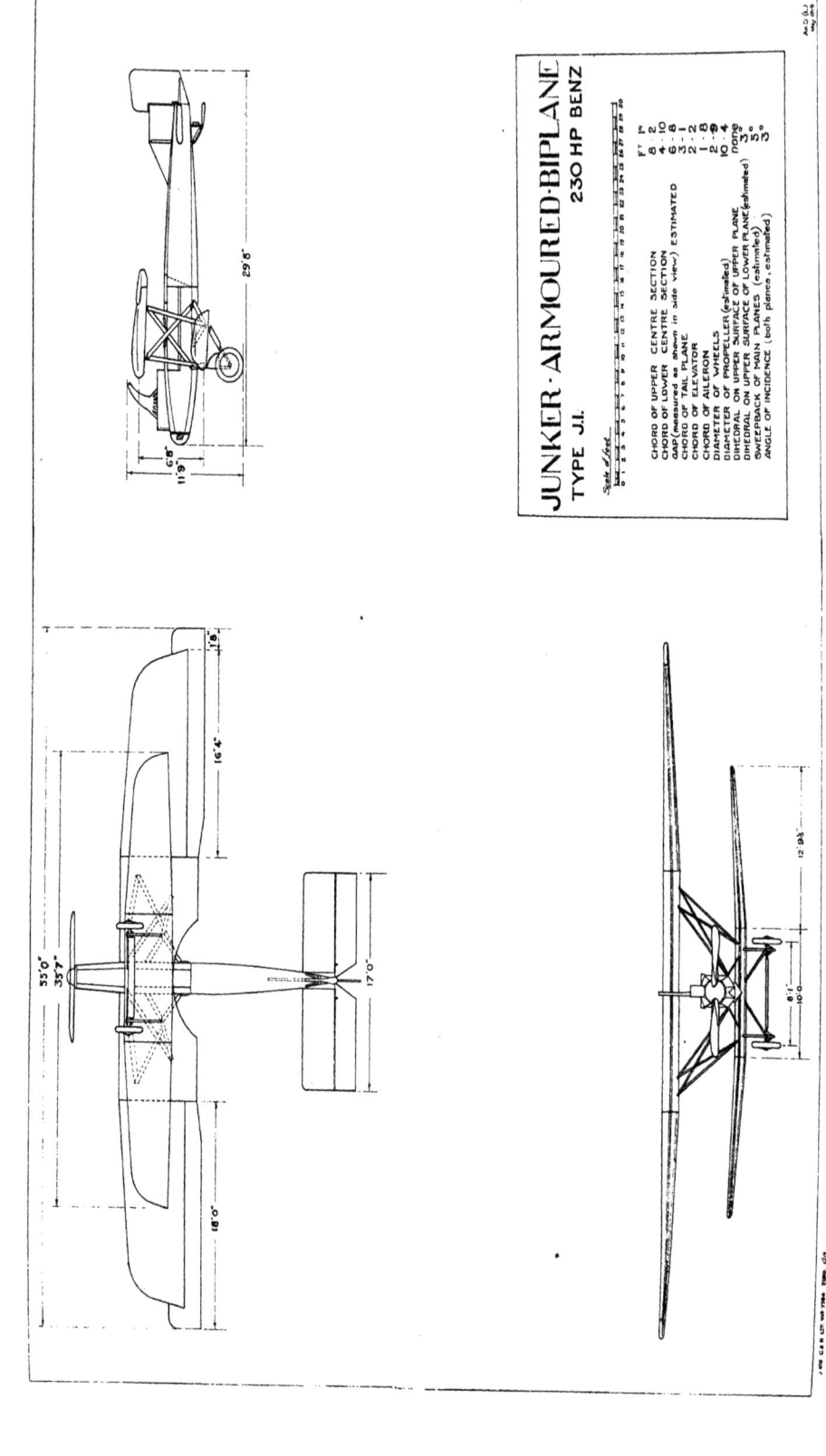

Report on the

JUNKER ARMOURED TWO-SEATER BIPLANE,

Type J.I.

Two machines have been examined, one of which was salved by British troops near La Vacquerie, during the German retreat. The other was brought down by the French. Armour-piercing bullets fired from a ground machine-gun penetrated the armour and caused the descent of the machine.

As the data upon which this report is based were collected from the debris of these two examples, both of which were entirely dismantled and greatly damaged, there are points upon which a certain amount of uncertainty must exist. The utmost care has been taken, however, in the reconstruction of the machine, and doubtful points are specified.

GENERAL.

The Junker is radically different from the usual type of aeroplane, whether considered from the point of view of design or of actual construction.

It is evidently a serious attempt to reduce to a minimum the dangers due to enemy action while in flight, and to lengthen the life and endurance of the machine in spite of exposure to bad weather and to rough handling. To this end the machine is armoured, and all vulnerable units, so far as possible, are gathered within the armoured portion. Inflammable materials, and those which suffer rapid deterioration when exposed to rough weather, are almost eliminated. Tension bracing by means of wire cable is entirely absent, rigidity in planes, fuselage, and undercarriage being obtained in all cases by metal tubes. Even the aileron control is without wiring, and careful search has failed to reveal any constructional wiring save that of the elevator and rudder controls.

No information is to hand regarding performance, but it is known that the machine requires an exceptionally long run before getting off.

GENERAL PARTICULARS AND DIMENSIONS.

Weights. (See table at end of report.) Figures painted on fuselage give :—

Weight, empty	3,724 lbs.
Useful weight	845 lbs.
Total weight	4,569 lbs.

Engine	230 H.P. Benz.
Crew	Two, pilot and observer-gunner.
Petrol Capacity	26 gallons.
Oil Capacity	10 gallons.
Weight per H.P.	19·9 lbs.
Loading per square foot	8·56 lbs.

Dimensions. (See scale drawings at end of report.)—

Area of upper centre section	134·7 sq. ft.
Area of each upper plane (with aileron)	125·8 sq. ft.
Area of complete upper wing (with ailerons)	386·3 sq. ft.
Area of each aileron	32·0 sq. ft.
Area of balance of aileron	2·4 sq. ft.
Area of lower centre section	48·0 sq. ft.
Area of each lower plane	49·6 sq. ft.
Area of complete lower wing	147·2 sq. ft.
Area of total wing surface	533·5 sq. ft.
Horizontal area of fuselage	52·1 sq. ft.
Vertical area of fuselage	76·0 sq. ft.
Area of fin	12·0 sq. ft.
Area of rudder	15·4 sq. ft.
Area of balance of rudder	1·6 sq. ft.
Area of fixed tail planes (both sides)	49·0 sq. ft.
Area of elevators (both)	33·6 sq. ft.

WINGS.

General Design.—The upper plane has a large centre section (rectangular except for the cut-away portion over the pilot's head), which is strongly braced to the fuselage by means of a system of steel tube struts. The leading edges of the upper planes are set back at an angle of approximately 5 deg. from the line of the centre section leading edge, but the trailing edges are at right angles to the line of flight for by far the greater part of their length.

The lower planes follow more or less the same plan, but the lower centre section is very much smaller than the upper and is built up in one unit with the undercarriage. To this unit the fuselage is firmly fixed by short steel tube struts, and an aluminium fairing is built around that part of the fuselage which is adjacent to the centre section's upper surface. There are apparently two attachments which directly couple the fuselage to the centre section unit. These take the form of lugs fitted to the two bottom edges of the octagonal body, midway between the forward pair of strut attachments. The lugs are bolted to corresponding lugs welded on to steel sleeves, which are in turn riveted to two upper duralumin spars of the lower centre section. The aluminium cowl which bridges the gap between body and lower centre section is simply a fairing. To each side of the lower centre section is fixed a side plane, which tapers in plan view from both front and rear, towards the tips. Reference to the plan view given in the scale drawing will make these points clear.

Fig. 1.

The damaged condition of the machines under examination has prevented absolute certainty on the question of dihedral, but there are excellent grounds for believing that the front view of the machine approximates very closely to the true disposition of the planes. It will be seen on reference to this view that the upper surface of the upper wings is horizontal, as in the D.7 Fokker, and on this point there is hardly any doubt. There is undoubtedly a dihedral on the lower planes, but the exact angle of dihedral is a matter of estimation. The angle given in the drawings, viz., 3 deg., is probably very near the truth. It will also be noticed from the scale drawings that the angle of incidence has been estimated at 3 deg. for both upper and lower planes.

The planes are based on the Fokker principle, *i.e.*, they are made sufficiently strong to obviate the necessity for external wire bracing.

The port and starboard planes, both upper and lower, depend entirely for their support upon the spar joints.

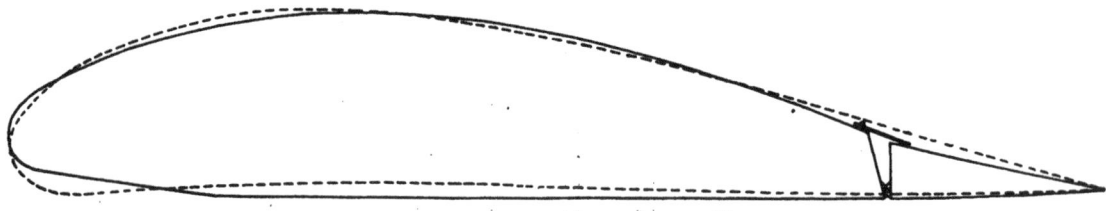

Fig. 2. *Note.*—The Fokker section is shown dotted.

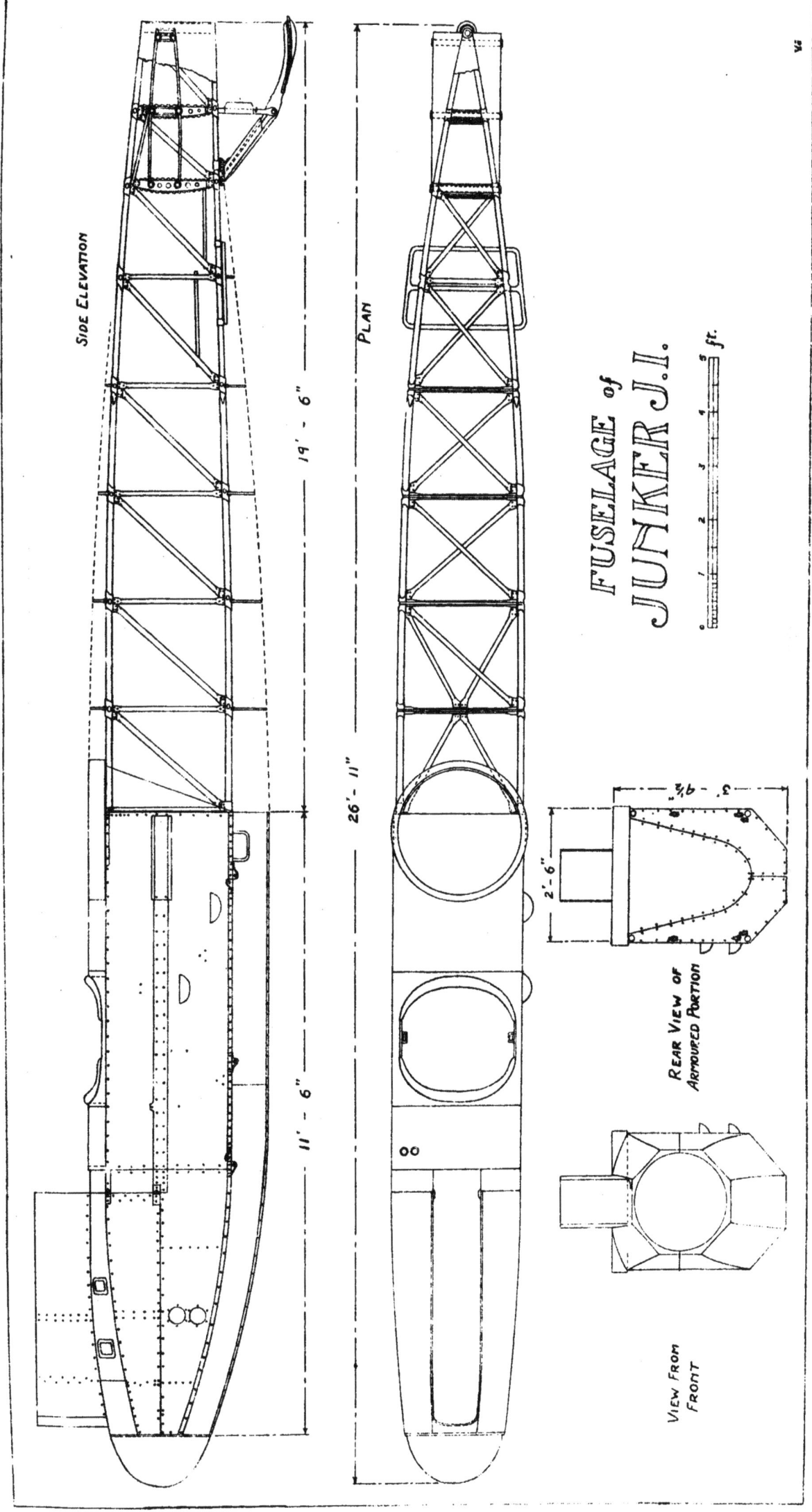

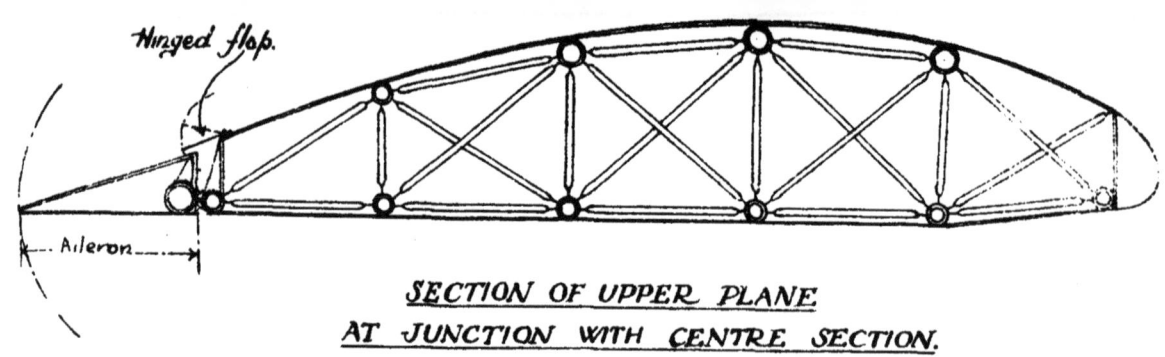

SECTION OF UPPER PLANE AT JUNCTION WITH CENTRE SECTION.

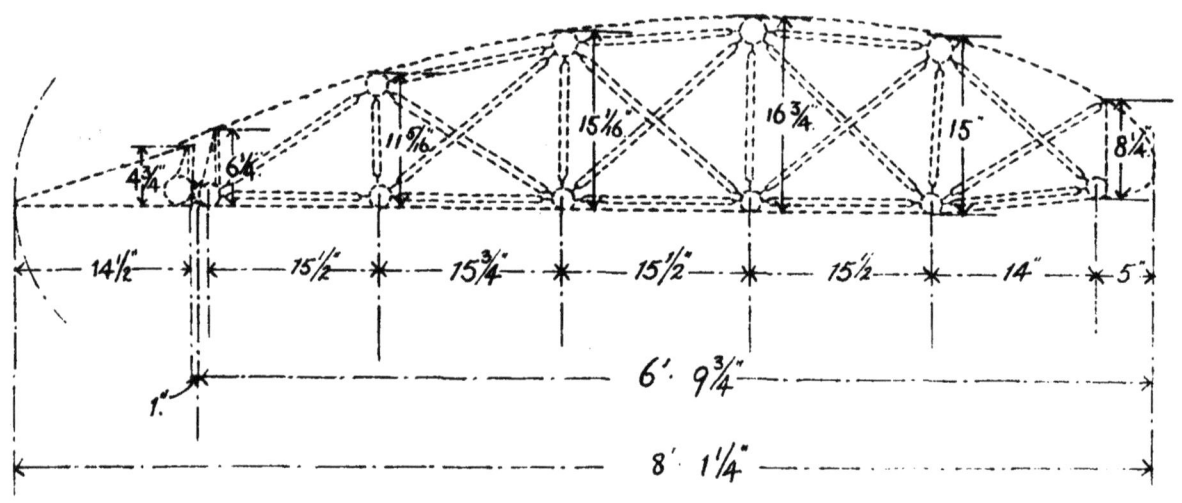

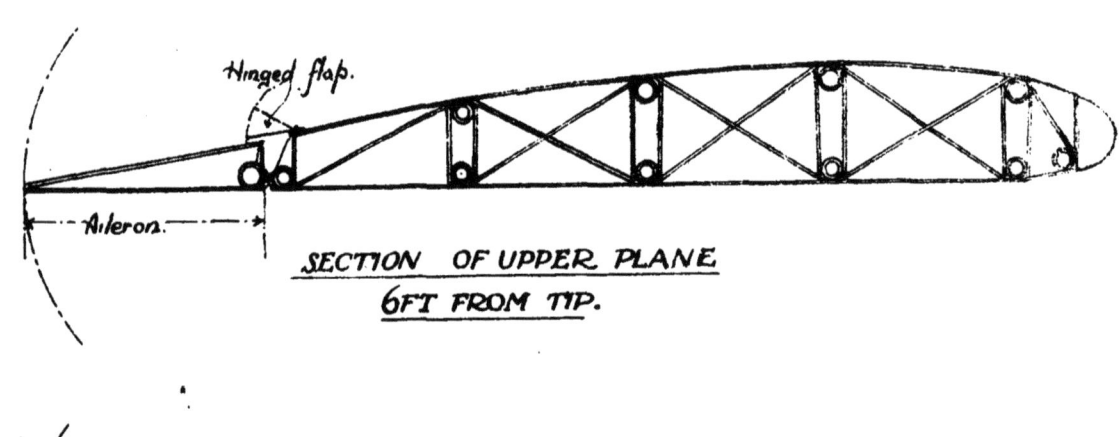

SECTION OF UPPER PLANE 6FT FROM TIP.

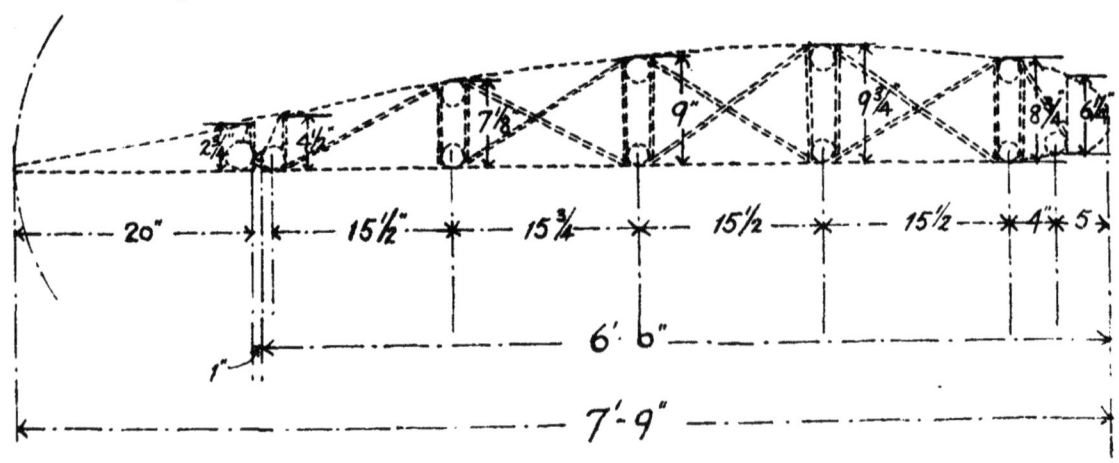

WING SECTION.

Sections drawn to scale are shown in Fig. 3 and on page 3, and Fig. 2 gives a comparison between the Junker J.I and Fokker D.VII aero-foil sections. There is a good deal of similarity between the two, but it must be remembered that the Junker wings are set at an appreciable angle of incidence, whereas the Fokker planes are without incidence.

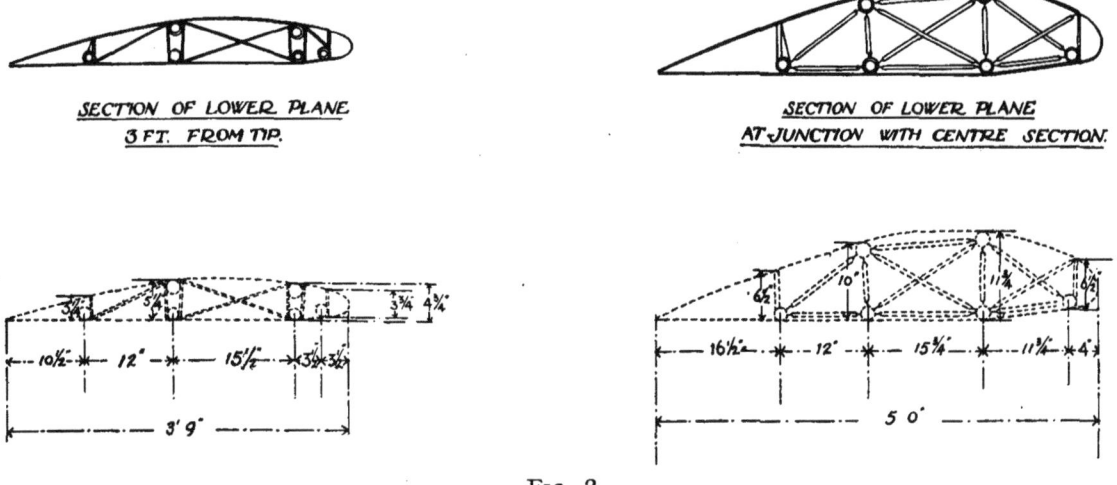

FIG. 3.

WING CONSTRUCTION.

It is in this particular that the greatest departure from established practice is found. The planes are constructed entirely of metal, even to the covering. A description of the constructional features of one of the upper planes will explain the system upon which the wings are built.

Each upper plane contains 10 spars of duralumin tube, without counting the aileron tube. Page 3 gives a section drawn to scale, showing the disposition of these spars, and the lower half of the diagram gives all dimensions, including the diameters and gauges of the tubes. The tubular spars are braced to each other by means of smaller tubes, also of duralumin. The exact system employed is shown very clearly in the photograph (Fig. 7) and the sketch (Fig. 8). It will be noticed that steel sleeves are riveted at intervals along the spars, and that the bracing tubes are flattened out at the ends and riveted to small flat plates welded on to the steel collars. Examples of these joints are given in Figs. 4 and 5.

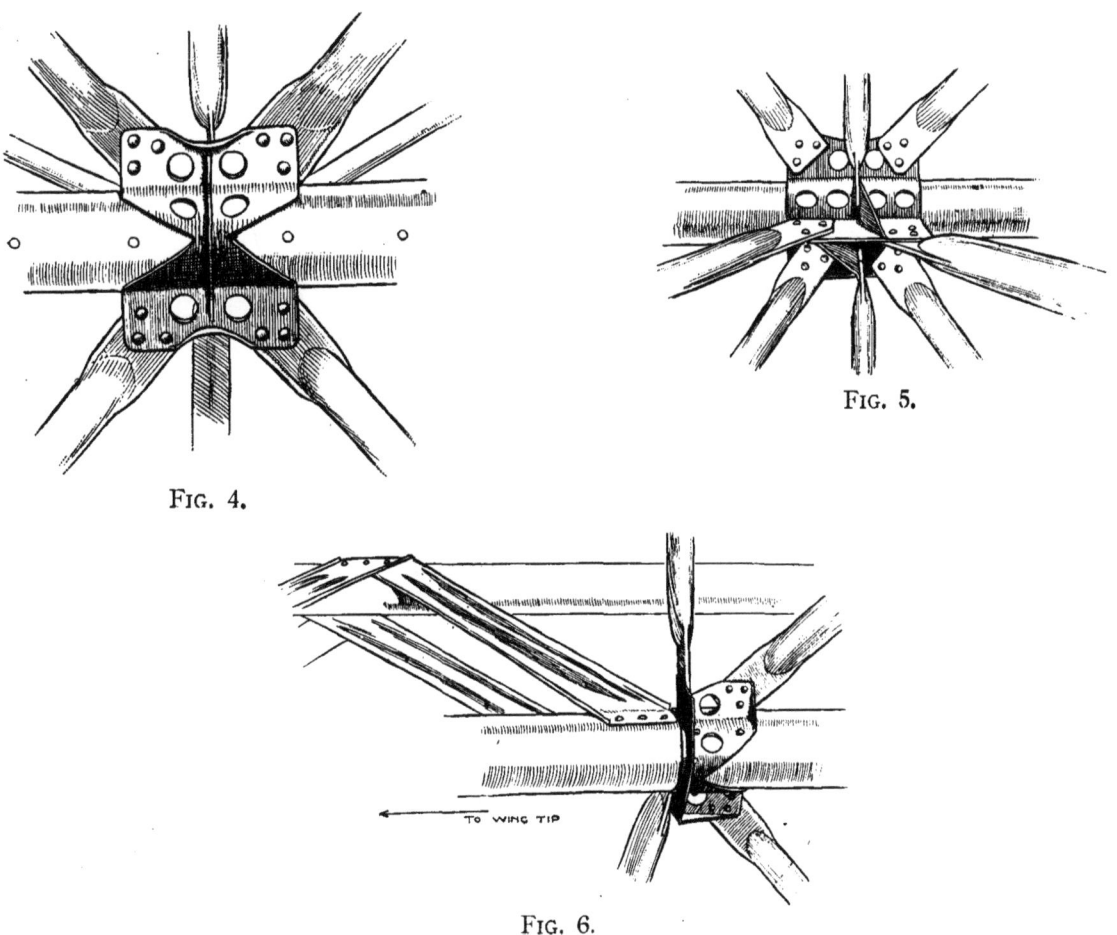

FIG. 4.

FIG. 5.

FIG. 6.

Fig. 7.

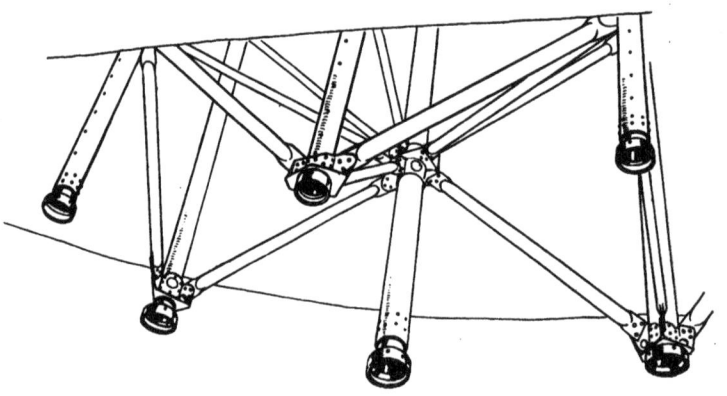

Fig. 8.

The constructional methods already described as being found in the upper planes are followed throughout both wings and centre sections except that towards the tips the place of the bracing tubes is taken by strips of duralumin longitudinally grooved to resist bending strains. Fig. 9 shows this, and also makes it clear that the steel collars to which the bracing tubes are riveted are not found where strips are employed. The finish of the tubular bracing and commencement of strip bracing is illustrated in Fig. 6.

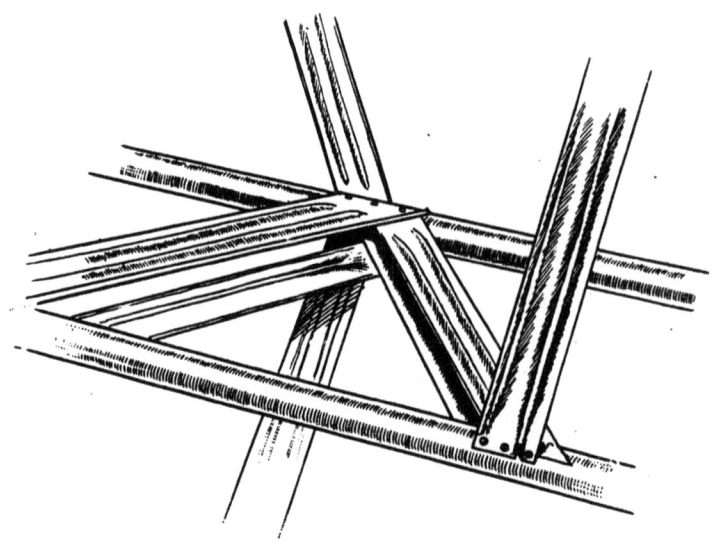

Fig. 9.

Some of the wing spars are spliced, a tube of larger diameter being joined to one of smaller diameter by being pressed into a square section as shown in Fig. 19, and riveted in place. It is not known whether liners are fitted at these places. The lower drawing of Fig. 19 shows how two portions of equal-sized tube are joined by means of a steel collar.

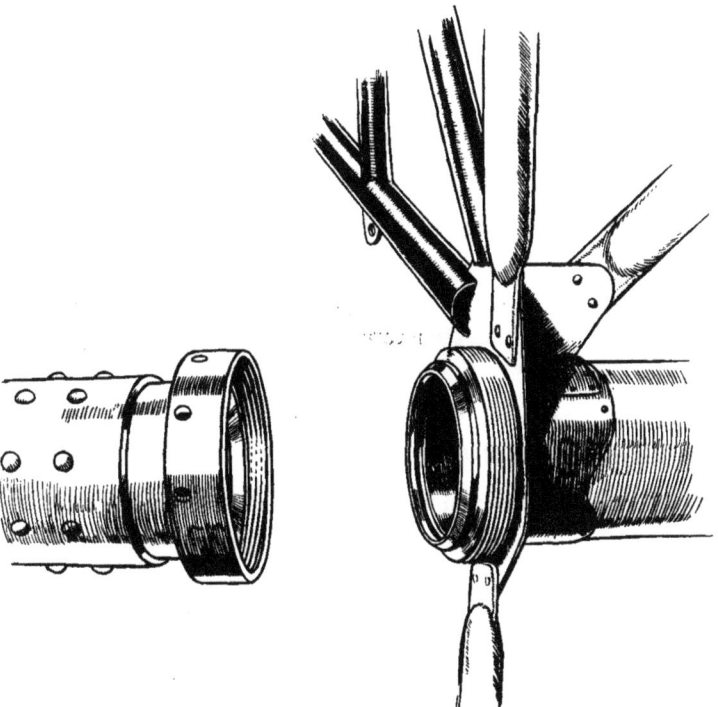

Fig. 15.

The way in which the wings are joined to the centre sections is simple and effective. Reference to Figs. 15 and 16 (which are not necessarily drawn to scale), shows that each of the spars is fitted with a steel sleeve which fits inside the duralumin tube and is riveted in place. One sleeve carries a threaded collar bevelled as shown. The opposite spar has a similar internal liner of steel, riveted in place, and a loose internally threaded steel collar. The end of the liner is bevelled to take the bevel of the opposite spar. Thus, when the bevels are fitted together, and the collar screwed on to the male thread (tommy holes can be seen in the sketch), a firm and rigid joint is made. When it is remembered that all the numerous tubes are joined in this manner, it is evident that the junction of wing to centre section is of great strength. Indeed, the designer has trusted solely to these joints to take all lift, drag, and landing strains, for there are no other attachments of any sort between wings and centre sections.

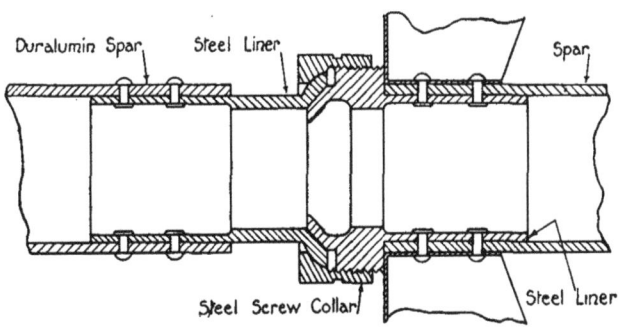

Fig. 16.

The sheet duralumin covering is ·015 in. thick (roughly 28 S.W.G.). It is corrugated so that a section cut parallel to the trailing edge is waved and the pitch of the wave is $1\frac{3}{4}$ in., the depth being $\frac{1}{3}$ in. The sheets are riveted together by aluminium rivets spaced at intervals of 1·8 in. The sheet weighs 3·65 oz. per sq. ft. of area, not allowing for lap in riveting. (It may be remarked that an approximate average weight for the usual German wing fabric, including dope, etc., is 1 oz. per sq. ft.)

Analysis of the material shows :—

Copper	4·46
Tin	Nil.
Lead	Trace.
Iron	0·60
Zinc	Nil.
Manganese	0·28
Magnesium	0·50
Silicon	0·39

This analysis shows that the material is "Duralumin."

PHYSICAL TESTS.

Test pieces cut from the sheet in two perpendicular directions gave :—

	A	B
Yield	18·2	18·1 tons per sq. in.
Ultimate	18·8	19·4 ,, ,, ,,
Elongation	3·3	3·3 per cent.
Reverse bends	3	3 ,,

These values correspond to a strength of 650 lbs. per in.

(The above figures are much below the requirements of Air Board specification for Duralumin sheet.)

MICRO-EXAMINATION.

The micro-structure shows that the sheet has apparently not been heat treated after rolling, the section showing the elongated crystalline structure characteristic of cold rolled material.

AILERONS.

It is evident from the scale drawings and photographs that the upper plane only is furnished with ailerons ; that the ailerons are of the balanced type ; and that each one reaches from the centre section to the wing tip.

The construction is simple. A duralumin tube passes from end to end, along the front lower edge, and to this is riveted the duralumin sheet which forms the lower surface of the aileron. A construction somewhat similar to that shown in Fig. 21 supports the upper sheet, and the two sheets are riveted together at the rear.

A hinged strip, about 4 ins. wide, and capable of moving upwards only, is fixed near the rear edge of the upper plane, thus bridging the gap between aileron and wing.

STRUTS.

The arrangement of struts is one of the most interesting features of the Junker biplane. Examination of the photographs will reveal the fact that there are three groups of struts.

1. Struts connecting upper plane to lower plane (marked A. and B. in photograph 10).
    There are two pairs of these ; one pair on each side of the body.
2. Struts connecting the upper extremities of A. and B. to the lower edge of the fuselage side (marked C. and D. in photograph).
    It will be noticed that these struts cross from front to rear, and that interference between the two is prevented by arranging that their upper extremities fall on different chords (*see* front view, general arrangement drawings).
3. Struts connecting the lower edge of the fuselage side to those points in the lower plane to which the undercarriage struts are fixed (marked E. F. G. in photograph).

Fig. 10.

Fig. 11.

All these struts are of steel tube covered with aluminium fairing. Steel formers are welded to the tube at intervals, and to these the fairing is riveted. The two edges of the fairing are turned in and joined together, at the narrow rear edge, by means of split pins. The longer tubes at least, and probably all, are of 4 cms. diameter and 15 gauge. They are joined to the spars by means of riveted steel collars carrying welded-on lugs.

At the fuselage, the struts finish in fork-ends, and are bolted to lugs welded to small steel plates riveted to the armour plate. These lugs are shown in Fig. 14.

FUSELAGE.

The body of the Junker is constructed in two distinct parts—a front armoured portion, and a rear portion built up of duralumin tubes.

The armoured part, the dimensions of which may be read from the drawing on page 4, is built of 5 mm. steel plate. The Junker is not an ordinary two-seater machine to which armour has been subsequently added, but the armour plate comprises the fuselage, as would be expected. The various photographs show clearly the shape of the body, also the number and size of the plates which are riveted together. A section of the fuselage is shown in Fig. 13. The bracing strips are made of duralumin.

The armoured unit houses the engine, pilot, and gunner, and the petrol tank. The vertical cowl surrounding the engine cylinders is of armour plate and is not a mere fairing. The spinner which covers the propeller boss is made of aluminium. The armouring is very thorough, so that the chances of a bullet finding a vulnerable spot are small.

Fig. 12 shows the rear of the armoured portion, together with the observer's seat.

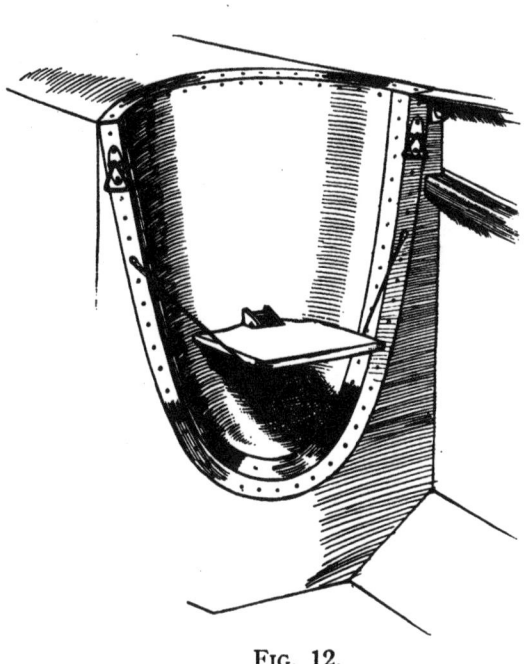

Fig. 12.

Figs. 13 and 14.

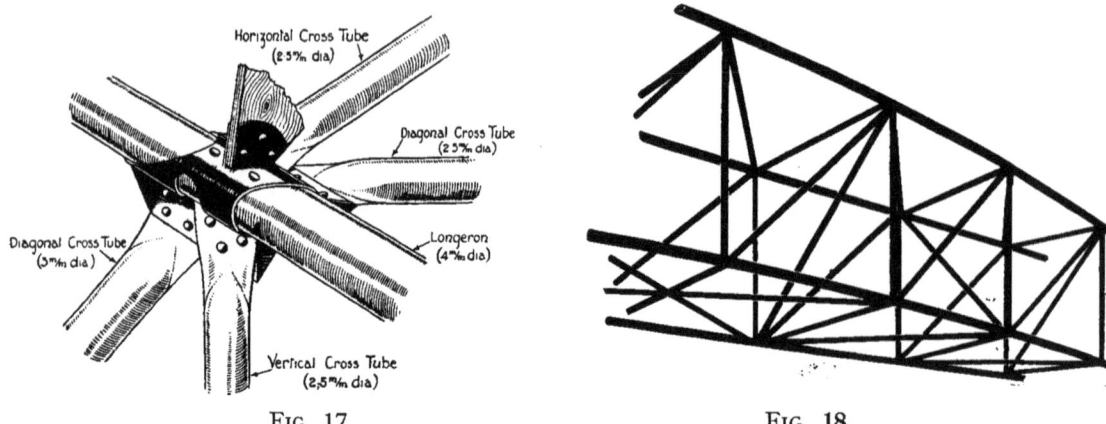

Fig. 17.   Fig. 18.

The rear portion of the body is built of duralumin tube throughout, and is covered with laced-on fabric. There are four longerons, so arranged that the fuselage ends in a vertical knife-edge about 16 in. long. Cross tubes are arranged horizontally and vertically at intervals. The diagonal bracing is not of wire, as is the case in the D.7 Fokker and the A.E.G. (which, it will be remembered, also have fuselages of metallic tubes). Diagonal tubes perform this function in the Junker. The arrangement of bracing tubes may be gathered from Fig. 18, and is worthy of careful attention.

The junction of the duralumin tubes is effected by means of steel sleeves which embrace the longerons tightly and are pinned to them. The exact shape of one of these clips is shown in Fig. 17. It will be noticed that the cross and diagonal tubes are flattened at their extremities, and riveted to appropriate shelves welded on to the clip. Three-ply formers are fixed to the upper and lower cross tubes, and (in the case of the deeper lower formers, at any rate), are joined by light wood stringers which pass from the end of the armoured portion to the front end of the tail skid.

The rear portion of the body is a structure of great strength. The vertical tubes in the last two bays before the stern-post are replaced by strong bulkheads of duralumin sheet. The construction is made clear on page 4, which shows that the upper and lower longerons on each side are joined by duralumin sheet of channel section, which is wider at the middle than at either end. A rectangular sheet of corrugated duralumin is riveted on either side of the vertical channel girder, and inside the box thus formed are two stout duralumin tubes, the extremities of which carry bevelled steel collars similar to those on the ends of the wing spars. The space between the duralumin tubes and the front corrugated sheet is bridged by two duralumin channels, riveted at the front to the corrugated sheet, and at the rear to the tubes.

This construction is repeated in the next bay, and at the rear the pair of horizontal tubes are firmly attached to the sternpost. All six horizontal tubes are of equal length, and the exposed portions are covered by a flat duralumin sheet, as indicated.

It will be noticed that the longerons are not of the same diameter throughout, but are spliced towards the rear of the fourth bay (counting from the armoured portion). The character of the splice is precisely similar to that employed in the wing spars described above, and illustrated below.

About 5 ft. from the sternpost the fuselage drawings indicate a kind of horizontal grid which is fixed to the lower longerons. This comprises a steel tube structure which takes no part in strengthening the fuselage, but is intended solely to provide handles for lifting the rear part of the body of the machine.

The two short tubes shown in the side view above and at each side of the handles are duralumin guides for the control cables. (See Page 4.)

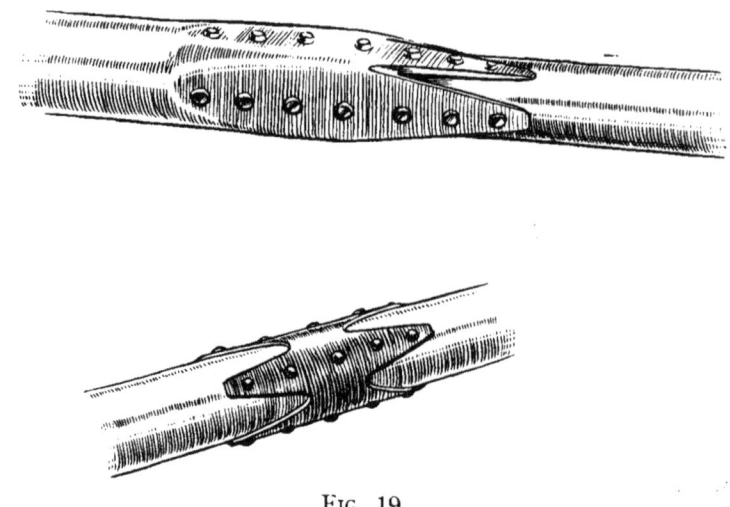

Fig. 19.

The junction of the two parts of the fuselage is very simple. From the outside, the longerons are seen to be butted up to the rear armour plate of the observer's cockpit, but no means of attachment is visible. Investigation from the interior of the cockpit shows that a substantial castellated steel nut is screwed over a steel bolt of about ½ in. diameter, and secured in place by the usual split pin. It was not possible to ascertain the exact manner of fixing the stud of the bolt into the end of the tubular longeron. Only the usual riveted steel collar to which the bracing tubes are riveted appears on the outside.

The drawing (Fig. 20), shows the principle of this arrangement.

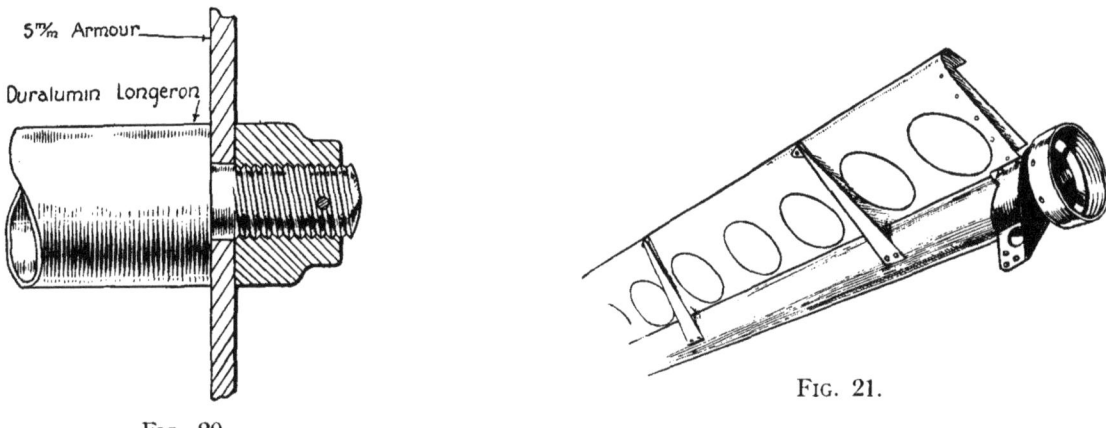

Fig. 20.

Fig. 21.

UNDERCARRIAGE.

This is built to form one unit with the lower centre section. There are two vees which are of normal design, except that a supplementary tube is welded to the upper extremity of the forward limb and to a point just below the middle of the rear tube (*see* Fig. 22). The vees are parallel and vertical. The shock absorbing device—of which a sketch may be seen in Fig. 22—does not present any unusual feature. Twin coil spring is employed and a double loop of cable limits the upward travel of the axle, while a radius rod controls the movements of the axle. It will be noticed also from Fig. 33 that each vee is stayed by means of a steel tube which connects the lower part of the front limb to the middle of the lower centre section, and that wire bracing is entirely absent.

The axle is a steel tube nearly 9 ft. long. In common with all other exposed tubes in the machine, it is faired with sheet aluminium, which is riveted to transverse webs (also of aluminium), which are in turn riveted to the axle tube. The fairing is therefore of the type that rises with the axle when the machine lands. There are no compression tubes fitted parallel to the axle, since the extra pair of tubes already mentioned render this unnecessary. Incidentally, they also eliminate wire-bracing. On other German aeroplanes which avoid wire wing-bracing (such as the D.7 Fokker and D.15 Pfalz) the undercarriage wires constitute the only external bracing.

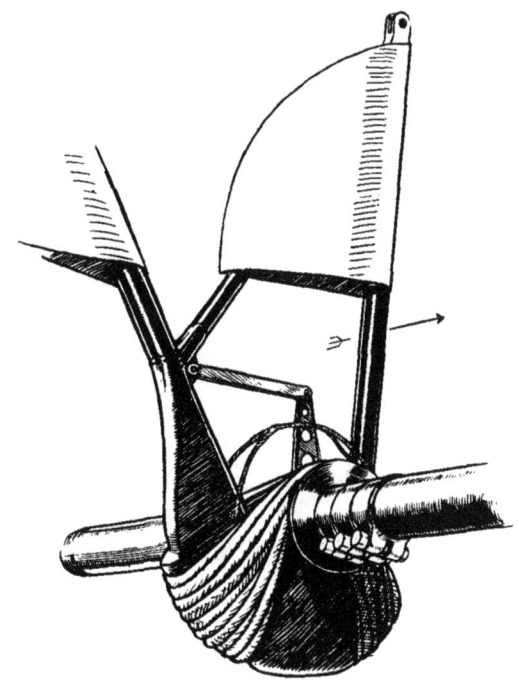

Fig. 22.

CONTROLS.

A diagram of the Junker control system is given in Fig. 23, and serves to show how anxious the designer has been to avoid wires as far as possible. The duralumin control lever is forked at its lower extremity and pivoted to a short cross-piece. Through the triangle thus formed passes a longitudinal rocking shaft, to which the cross-piece is fixed by a short tube. The duralumin rocking shaft carries a steel sleeve to which is welded a light steel beam ending in a fork on each side. This constitutes part of the aileron control, which is worked by means of linked tubes, as in the Nieuport scout and the Halberstadt fighter. Tubes are carried up from the fork ends of the crossbeam to the ends of two shorter levers, one on each side, and vertical steel tubes pass up from these levers to the upper plane. Fig. 26 gives an excellent idea of the joy stick, and several of the photographs clearly show the vertical tubes passing from fuselage to upper wing.

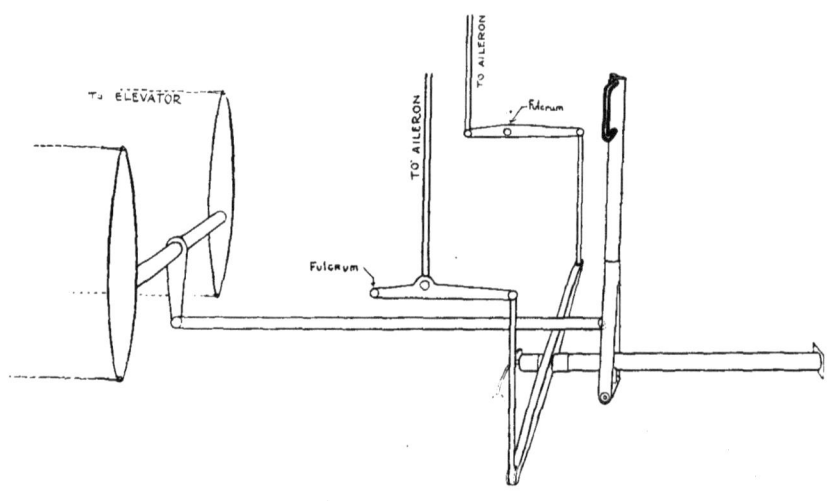

Fig. 23.

Two duralumin tubes pass through the upper centre section, parallel to the spars. They are placed end to end in the same straight line, and pass immediately in front of the third pair of tubular spars (counting from the leading edge). Short cranks fitted to steel collars are riveted to each of these tubes and to the aileron hinge tube, and a steel tube of 25 mm. diameter connects these levers. At a distance of 7 ft. 3 in. from this arrangement another crank is riveted to each tube, and one of the vertical tubes from the fuselage is connected to this crank. Fig. 24 shows the whole arrangement, for one side, in perspective.

Examination of Fig. 23 will reveal the strange fact that the horizontal levers to which the aileron control rods are attached are not of the same order. The port side lever has the fulcrum between the two ends, while the pivot of the starboard lever is at one end. The effect of this would be, of course, to cause both the aileron rods to travel in the same direction. Thus, if the joy stick were inclined to port, both rods would rise, while a starboard inclination of the lever would cause the rods to fall. It is not known whether this is found in all Junker J.1 machines, nor by what means the movement is reversed on one side between controls and ailerons.

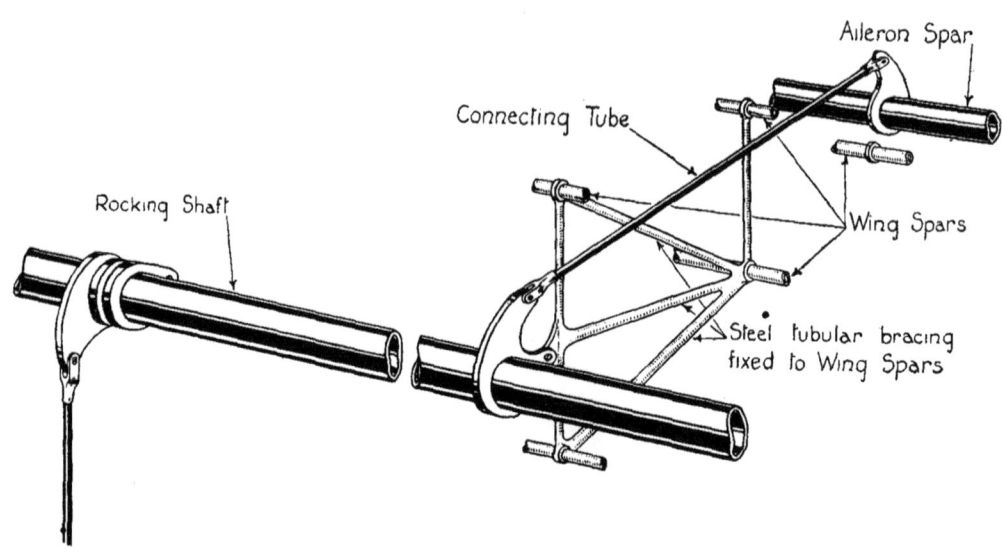

Fig. 24.

The Junker elevators are controlled by means of stranded cables attached to vertical levers, which are actuated by a steel tube direct from the control column. The extremities of the two vertical levers are not equidistant from the pivotal tube, but the upper part of each is appreciably greater than the corresponding lower part. It is found that the upper and lower portions of the elevator kingposts bear the same relation to one another, and the idea is evidently to reduce the mechanical strain on the upper control wire.

The rudder control embodies a curved steel tubular rudder bar, as shown in Fig. 25, and the customary cables and pulleys. Neither stirrups nor adjustment of position are provided. Two pairs of kingposts are fitted to the rudder post, and the cables are duplicated.

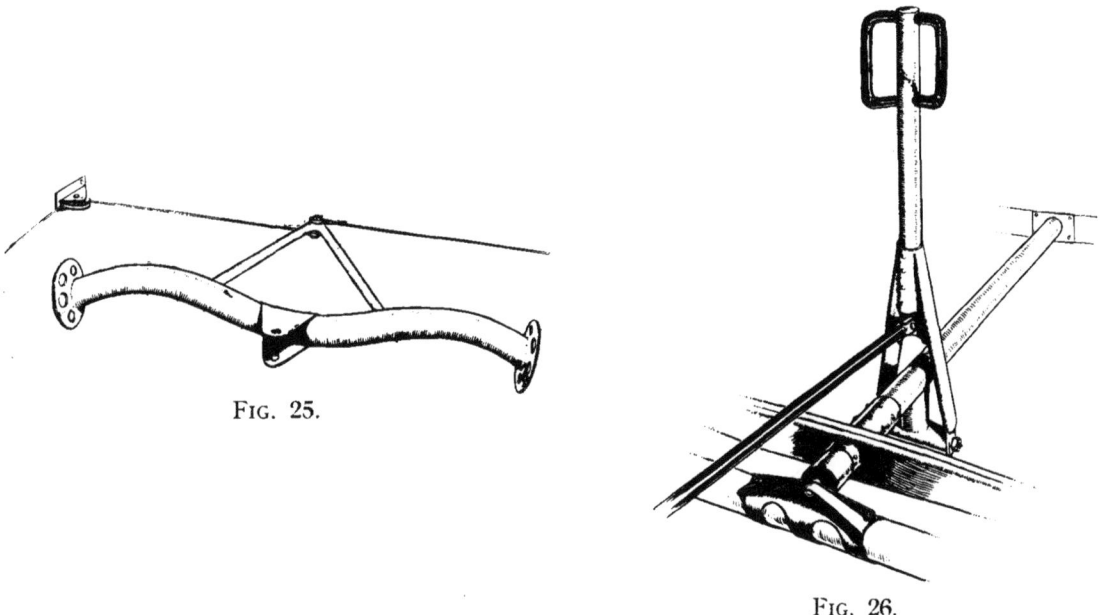

Fig. 25.

Fig. 26.

TAIL.

The rear portion of the fuselage has already been described, and mention has been made of six short horizontal tubes which finish in steel screw-collars. The two halves of the fixed tail plane are held in position solely by these joints. The section of the tail plane is of approximately the same shape as that of the wing. It contains seven tubular spars—one single tube in front, and three pairs at intervals behind, and the greatest depth is approximately $7\frac{1}{4}$ in. The covering is exactly similar to that of the wings, as also is the internal construction. The front spar is not fixed in any way to the fuselage, and the front foot or so of the tail plane simple abuts against the fabric.

The construction of the divided elevator is very simple. At the front is a duralumin tube hinged by the means shown in Fig. 27 to the rear edge of the tail plane. There are six such hinges altogether—three to each half of the elevator. The corrugated duralumin covering is riveted to the spar and is also held together at its rear edge by rivets.

The shapes of the fin and balanced rudder may be gathered from the scale drawings and the various photographs. There are two tubular stays from the upper longerons to the apex of the fin. The rudder consists of a tube, a U-shaped leading edge of plain duralumin sheet, and two halves of corrugated duralumin, riveted together at the rear edge. The rudder depends for its strength therefore solely on the covering; and this is probably true of the fin also.

The tail skid is a substantial piece of ash bound with fabric, pivoted about its middle point, and fitted at the lower extremity with a welded steel shoe. The shock absorber consists of the usual steel coil spring. The four tubes which carry the tail skid are in the form of a pyramid, and are composed of steel. The fairing is of sheet steel welded on, which adds considerably to the strength of the structure.

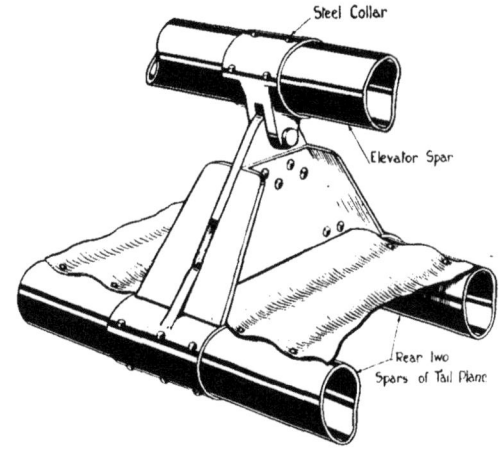

Fig. 27.

ENGINE AND ENGINE MOUNTING.

The engine installed is a 230 H.P. Benz, and it is remarkable that in such an all-metal type of machine the engine bearers are of ash. The bearers have sheet steel supports, and are braced to the side by means of duralumin tubes of 20 mm. diameter. Fig. 29 shows how this is done. The petrol tank is an elaborate structure of sheet brass. As shown in Fig. 28, it is built up into the form of an armchair, and is capable of carrying 26 gallons. The horizontal tunnel running from front to back accommodates the elevator control tube. Near the position of the pilot's right shoulder can be seen the top of the cylindrical pressure tank which is part of the well-known Benz petrol system.

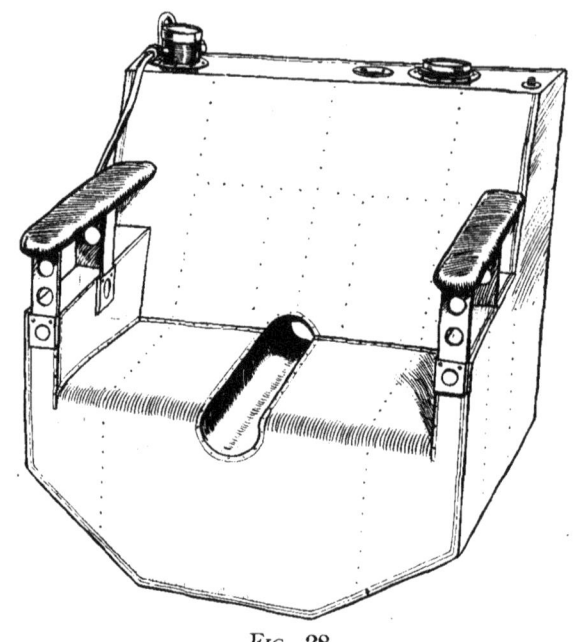

FIG. 28.

The oil tank is reported to have been carried just in front of the instrument board, and to have a capacity of 10 gallons.

Two different forms of exhaust pipes have been noticed, discharging above and in front of the upper plane; both types are frequently used with 230 H.P. Benz engines.

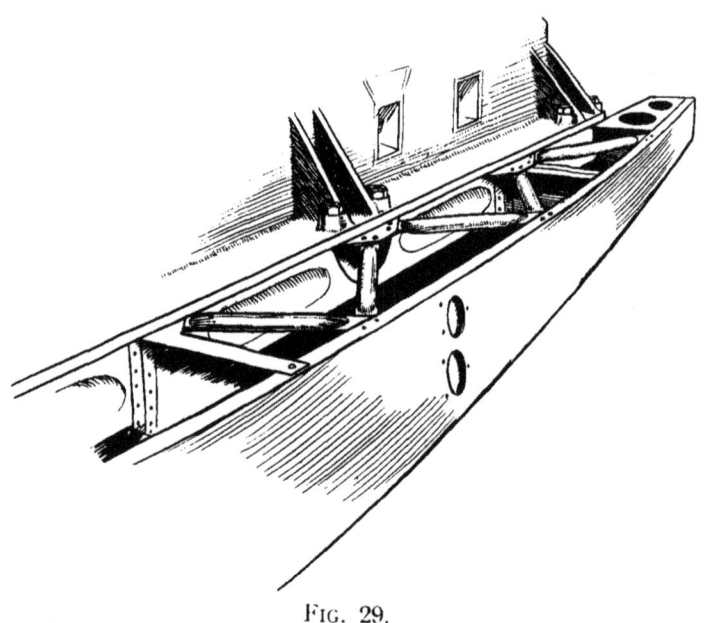

FIG. 29.

RADIATOR.

A drawing of the radiator found with other damaged parts of the Junker biplane is given on page 14. According to the evidence of the photographs it was fixed to the lower surface of the upper plane, over the rear part of the engine.

An aluminium box surrounds the radiator on all sides except front and rear, and the cooling effect is controlled by flaps hinged at their lower edge to the front and rear of the box. The setting of this elementary type of shutter could not be altered during flight.

It will be noticed that the water flows through a broad and shallow horizontal ribbon-tube, the zig-zags of thin brass being merely distance pieces.

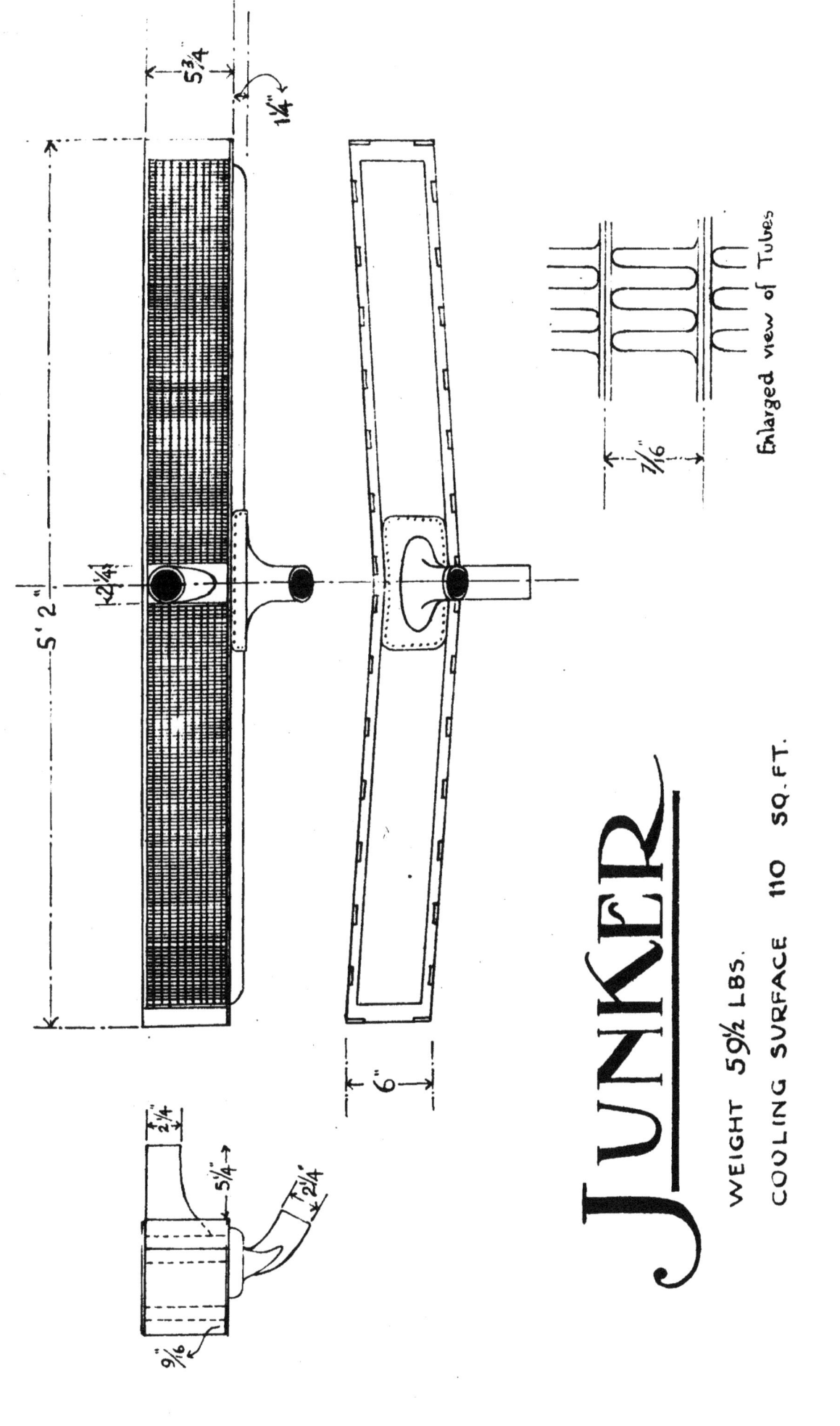

ARMAMENT.

It is known that no Spandau or other gun was fixed to be controlled by the pilot and to fire forward; also that the observer's gunring carried a Parabellum gun on the usual type of mounting.

No traces of guns fixed to fire downward were found on either of the machines examined, but it is known that many Junker biplanes carried two Parabellum guns immovably fixed in parallel positions on the left of the observer, firing downwards and forwards through holes in the fuselage armour and in the lower centre section. Other J.1. Junker biplanes are known to have been fitted with wireless, but no machine has been known to carry both wireless and extra fixed guns.

Very lights were carried in an aluminium rack on the side of the fuselage.

COLOURING.

The machine is thinly painted in matt colours. The upper surface of the planes has irregular masses of the usual green and mauve tints, while the underside is painted a bluish-white colour. The struts and wheels are green, as is the armoured portion of the fuselage.

INSTRUMENTS.

None were salved. A circular well, which presumably accommodated the compass, may be seen in the photographs, in the starboard side of the lower centre section.

TABLE OF APPROXIMATE WEIGHTS.

Upper centre section	198 lbs.
One upper plane without aileron	165 lbs.
One aileron	$30\frac{1}{4}$ lbs.
One lower plane	63 lbs.
Main petrol tank	54 lbs.
Radiator	60 lbs.

G.T.C. (Ap. D.(L)).

R. BROOKE-POPHAM,
Brigadier-General,
Director of Research.

May, 1919.

Fig. 30.—View of Complete Machine—from a German Source.

Fig. 31.—Front View of Machine—from a German Source.

Fig. 32.—Rear View taken from a Damaged Machine in Belgium.

Fig. 33.—The Lower Centre Section-cum-Undercarriage Unit.

Fig. 34.—Side View of a Wrecked Machine.

APPENDIX.

The following is a translation of a German Instruction Manual for the Junker biplane. It was not available when the text of the report was prepared, but is included because it amplifies the text in several important particulars.

Special attention is directed to the descriptions of the petrol system, the radiator, and the W/T installation. As pointed out in the actual report, the machines have been found to carry either a W/T outfit (sending and receiving) or, alternatively, two fixed machine guns firing downwards and forwards.

The paragraph on repairs refers twice to a special riveting apparatus. It is hoped to obtain particulars of this system, which allows good riveting to be carried out under conditions of extraordinary difficulty.

INSTRUCTION MANUAL FOR JUNK. J.I. ARMOURED BIPLANE.

JUNKERS—FOKKER—WERKE A.G. DESSAU.

Advantages of the Junkers type of Metal Aeroplane with Unbraced Wings.

STRENGTH.

In spite of the absence of struts and bracing wires, a high degree of safety is obtained with the Junkers construction.

The results of the loading test carried out by the P.U.W. der Fliegertruppen (Testing section and workshop of the Air Service), gave a margin of safety 30 per cent. higher than the required value (5·8 factor of safety).

The machines can withstand the most powerful stresses. For instance, the breakage of a wheel having caused a machine to turn turtle, only the tubular framework of the wings was damaged, the machine not being wrecked completely.

BULLET-PROOF QUALITIES.

The wing construction does not include any member which, if damaged might endanger the safety of the whole. The liability of this machine to damage of any kind caused by projectiles is therefore extraordinarily low.

SAFETY AGAINST FIRE.

These machines, including rudders and fins, being almost entirely constructed of non-inflammable material, are impervious to incendiary bullets or fires started in the carburetter.

SPEED.

The unbraced wings and the narrow fuselage without struts and bracing wires, which all add to the head resistance of the machine, enable the highest possible percentage of the engine power to be applied to increased speed and climb.

FIELD OF VISION.

The absence of struts and bracing wires, and the favourable arrangement of the wings, enable a very good view to be obtained.

AVAILABILITY FOR SERVICE.

This machine requires no rigging, and therefore no trueing up is necessary. No distortion occurs, even after a long period of exposure to the weather.

USES AND PROPERTIES OF THE ARMOURED BIPLANE.

The armoured biplane is a machine specially constructed for the requirements of infantry contact work.

Special attention has, therefore, been paid to the protection of the engine, crew and wireless. The weight of the armouring is 470 kg. and, therefore, the climb of this machine is low as compared to a fighter machine, and it requires a longer run at starting and landing.

Owing to the aerodynamic qualities of the thick unbraced wings, this machine possesses a high speed and an excellent gliding capacity.

As regards the equipment, special attention has been paid to obtain a convenient and simple arrangement of the fittings.

Preference is given to the W/T apparatus over the armament.

ARMOURING.

The armouring consists of a casing (open only at the top) of highly tempered special steel 5 mm. thick, made by the well-known "Panzerwerke" of Dillingen. This armouring is an efficient protection against rifle fire and shrapnel at the closest possible range. The armoured casing weighs 470 kg.

The engine armouring comes up to the top of the engine.

The engine, pilot, observer, fuel tanks, W/T apparatus, ammunition and part of the controls, are all within the armoured casing.

Any parts of the control outside the armouring are all duplicated.

ENGINE INSTALLATION.

A 6-cylinder 200 H.P. Benz engine* is used (see description of action and fuel supply system issued by the Benz firm of Mannheim.)

FITTING.

The fitting is so carried out that the engine can be uncovered on all sides, in spite of extensive armouring of the upper part, by means of hinged panels, easily opened. The bolts of the front panel eliminate any possibility of an accidental opening. The positions of the bolts are shown by coloured signs. Hinged panels, easily and quickly opened, are provided for inspection of the carburetter and oil pump.

The supply of air to the carburetter and crank case is carried out by means of special wind traps and supply pipes.

FUEL SUPPLY SYSTEM.

The fuel supply system ensures the greatest possible reliability.

The necessary controls are reduced to a single control cock I fitted on the instrument board.

In order to start the engine, control cock I is placed in position 1 as shown on the diagram, and petrol is pumped into the gravity tank by means of the hand pump until the petrol gauge shows that the gravity tank is full.

The engine is then started, the control cock being put at position 2. When the petrol pressure gauge registers a working pressure of about $\frac{1}{5}$ of an atmosphere (the pressure can be regulated by means of the adjusting screw of the relief valve), the control cock is put at position 3. In the case of fire in the carburetter, and when at rest, control cock I should be at position 4.

In case of a breakdown of the engine pump, the gravity tank is switched in by putting the control cock at position 2. As the gravity tank contains about 30 litres, the machine can fly on it for at least half-hour at full throttle.

Refilling of the gravity tank is carried out either through the excess pressure of the engine pump, or by means of the hand-pump, the control cock being at position 1.

Should the gravity petrol tank have become quite empty owing to a breakdown of the engine pump, it is still possible to supply the engine with fuel by continuous use of the hand pump, the control cock being placed at position 3.

The main petrol tank is divided into two separate compartments by means of a vertical partition, so that the whole tank does not empty should one of the compartments be damaged.

In such cases, it is possible to cut out the damaged compartment of the tank, by means of the three-way cock on the right side of the fuselage, so that the fuel is only taken up from the undamaged compartment (see diagram of petrol supply system).

* Actually 230 H.P

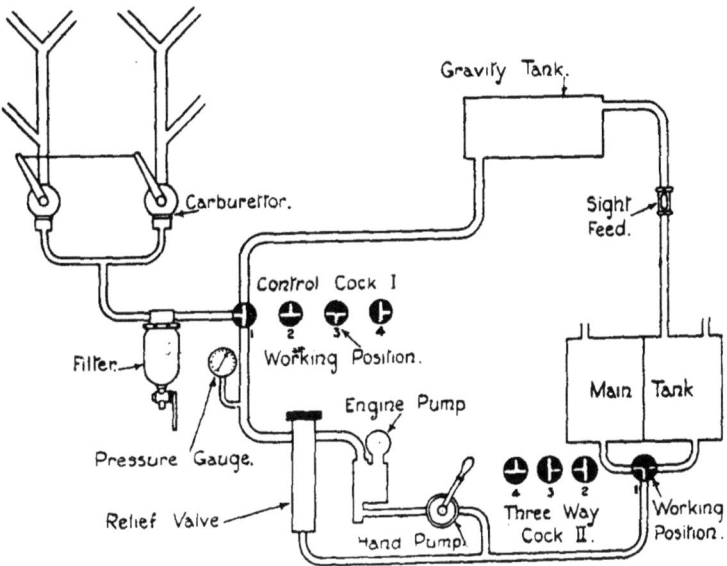

PETROL SUPPLY SYSTEM.

Two drain cocks are fitted near the bottom of the rear wall of the double tank by which the main tank can be emptied rapidly.

The gravity tank is emptied by the drain cock in the bottom of the petrol filter.

PROPELLER.

The machine carried out its flight test with a propeller constructed by the Axial-Propellerwerke of Berlin. According to the latest experiments a propeller 2·94 m. in diameter and with a pitch of 1·90 m. revolving at 1,380 to 1,400 r.p.m. on the test bench has been found suitable.

RADIATOR.

These machines are fitted with a jet radiator of the Junkers type, with a hood open back and front which decreases the head-resistance of the radiator.

The adjustable sections of the hood are regulated by means of an adjusting screw fitted at the side, according to the temperature of the surrounding atmosphere.

During the hot summer months, a maximum opening of the hood should be given, but during the cold weather the opening should be proportional to the temperature. The amount of the opening should be the same back and front.

The opening of the hood should be so regulated that the temperature of the cooling water does not exceed 75 deg. to 80 deg. The action of the radiator can be ascertained at all times by means of a thermometer fitted in the cooling system. Care should be taken that after each preliminary run before starting, the water tank is refilled, as not till this has been done can it be safely assumed that the whole water system is completely filled.

CONTROL SYSTEM.

The controls are primarily worked by the control column, the action of which is transmitted to the main control shaft and ailerons by means of a system of rods to which the controlling surfaces answer very easily. The rudders and ailerons are partly balanced. An adjustable double compensating spring takes up the weight of the elevator in such a way that when at rest the tension on the control column is about 2·5 kg.

The control column should have only slight play in its central position. This is rendered necessary by the type of control system used. The ailerons and elevators are constructed of metal and are therefore fire-proof. Should the fuselage covering be burnt away the machine could still be controlled.

W/T.

Special care has been taken to fit the W/T apparatus so that it can be worked conveniently. The standard "Telefunken" apparatus for both sending and receiving (specification 99) is fitted to this machine. The dynamo is easily accessible and adjustable. It is partly armoured. The length of the aerial is fixed at 37 m. for the "Telefunken" sender and at 38 m. for the "Huth" sender.

ARMAMENT.

A "Parabellum" machine gun is fitted in the observer's cockpit on a rotary turret. Three ammunition drums are fitted to the right and left of the observer's seat and are easily accessible. Two more drums are fitted under the seat. One thousand rounds can be carried altogether.

CAMERAS.

From series No. 101/17 upwards, these machines are provided with the necessary fittings for cinematograph cameras, hand camera and magazines.

The first bay of the fuselage behind the armour is made easily accessible from above and below by means of sliding or removable panels in the sheet metal armouring. The cinematograph camera is suspended from underneath. The dynamo should be fitted on the cabane to the left of the fuselage. Switch, regulating resistance, and voltmeter should be screwed to the ply-wood lining of the left side of the fuselage, in place of the front map carrier, so as to be easily accessible to the observer.

The conductors are led to the engine outside the armouring, through holes provided for the purpose. A bag for the hand camera is strapped in the first bay of the fuselage, above the cinematograph camera.

Sheet metal boxes are provided to take the magazines.

SIGNALLING APPARATUS.

A pocket is provided on either side of the fuselage to carry the supply of the usual lights, each pocket holding 10 lights.

CARE AND HANDLING OF MACHINE.

GENERAL.

When carrying out any work on the machines the following points should be observed :—

The wings and tail plane are covered with light metal sheeting $\frac{3}{10}$ mm. thick, the strength of which is quite sufficient to bear normal flying stresses, but, like fabric, cannot stand a heavy load over a small area.

Care should, therefore, be taken not to stand on or lean against these surfaces, and that no heavy article with sharp edges such as petrol tins, etc., are placed upon them. Never move the machine by pressing on the struts.

When moving the wings or the whole machine care should be taken to handle the wings with the palms of both hands as far as possible in the centre of the riveted joint. When storing wings, always lay them on a layer of straw or wood shavings, previously prepared and as level as possible.

The wings very soon become dented if this is not done. These dents are not a source of danger but a loss of time is incurred by their removal, which requires a certain skill. Moreover, this operation cannot be often repeated and always spoils the look of the machine.

TRANSPORT.

A fuselage truck 10 m. in length, and a truck for the various parts 7 m. in length, are required for transport by rail. The fuselage is loaded as a complete unit but without undercarriage or tail planes. The wings, struts, and tail surfaces are packed separately in wooden crates or cases. The fuselage can also be towed on its undercarriage by a tractor in the usual way.

ASSEMBLY.

Assembly should, if possible, take place in a shed with a roof strong enough to bear the weight of the top wing (about 250 kg.).

Should this not be possible the wing can be raised on high wooden trestles. When unpacking the various parts they should be placed in their proper position round the fuselage (see diagram).

The time required for assembling the machine varies with the number of men available. With six to eight men the machine should be ready for flight in four to six hours according to the appliances available. The work should be carried out by two groups, four to six men at the wings and two to three men fitting the tail surfaces.

If the radiator is not already fitted to the centre section of the top wing it should be screwed on and secured first of all. The two top wings must be screwed and secured to the centre section simultaneously.

Special spanners are supplied to fit the nuts of the connecting pieces. The aileron control rods are then fitted.

Ropes should be slung round the uncovered points of attachment of the tubular framework and the whole drawn up sufficiently high for the fuselage to be slipped underneath. Whilst the struts are being fitted and secured the two bottom wings are fitted in the same way as the top wing. The points of attachment can then be covered. The pipes of the cooling system must also be fitted.

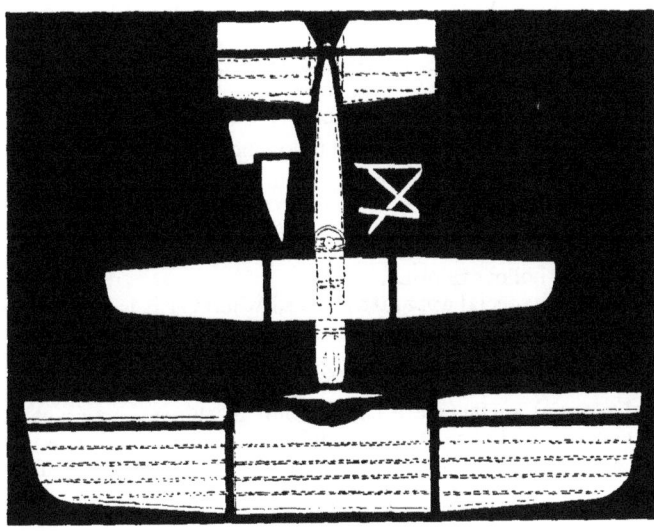

During this time the second group should have fitted and secured the tail planes (the connecting pieces are similar to those of the wings) followed by the fin, elevator and rudder. Finally the strut sockets in the bottom wing and the points of attachment of the wings and fixed tail surfaces should be covered and the control cables inserted and secured.

DISMANTLING.

The machine is dismantled in the reverse order.

Both during erection and dismantling the centre of balance of the machine should always be kept in view. Should there be any uncertainty concerning the position of the centre of gravity owing to the removal of one of the larger parts, it is advisable to load the tail skid with sand bags to avoid the danger of the machine turning turtle.

When the machine is not in use it is advisable to support the armoured casing on a trestle to take the weight of the machine off the spring of the tail skid. The trestles supplied should be used to remove the load on the undercarriage shock absorbers.

MAINTENANCE.

As already mentioned no rigging is necessary with this machine. Examine the capped nuts of all connecting pieces at regular intervals to make sure there is no working loose.

The wing covering and tubular frame-work are rust-proof, the object of the coating being merely to render the machines less visible.

Any parts of the control system liable to friction, such as pins and bearings, should be lubricated with a few drops of oil during assembly and subsequently at regular intervals. Special instructions are issued for the care of the engine and W/T apparatus.

In trestling up, the machine must never, as is sometimes done elsewhere, *be supported or raised by the wings. Only the trestles supplied may be used for trestling up the machine.*

REPAIRS.

Repairs to wings and tail of this machine require totally different materials from those required for ordinary machines.

Extensive repairs are hardly possible at the front or at aviation parks. The most rapid method of repairing damages is by obtaining the required spare parts. Trained mechanics can be had at any time for instruction purposes, when required.

A tool box and a case containing a supply of materials is supplied with each machine so that small repairs can be carried out quickly on the spot.

A list of contents is given in all the boxes.

The frame-work mainly consists of longitudinal members in light metal tubing, iron connections, and light metal tubular or Z struts. Damaged longitudinal members can be repaired by cutting away the dented or torn section of tubing near the connection and replacing it by a new section. A previously prepared sleeve is slipped over the join and fastened by means of four rows of rivets.

Damaged struts are entirely replaced and riveted to the connecting pieces in the usual way.

Connecting pieces and sleeves are fixed to the tubing by internal riveting, for which a special tool is used.

REPAIRING DAMAGED COVERING.

Damaged parts of the metal covering are cut away as near as possible to the lateral seams and longitudinal members. This must only be undertaken when it is necessary to repair part of the framework (cf. sketch).

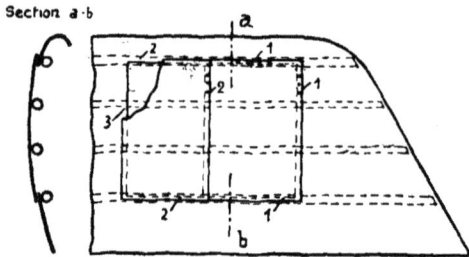

The covering of these surfaces is carried out in the following order according to the sketch above.
1. Fit the new corrugated sheet metal.
2. Rivet seam 1—1 in the usual way.
3. Rivet seam 2—2.
4. Rivet seam 3—3 in the usual way.
5. Rivet seam 4—4 by hollow riveting.

Hollow riveting by means of a special apparatus is used wherever it is impossible to use a holding-up device, as in ordinary riveting.

REPAIRING DAMAGE TO TAIL SURFACES.

Repairs to the metal covered surfaces are carried out as above. In cases of extensive damage, it is advisable to order a new part. Fabric covered surfaces are repaired in the usual way. Small slits in the sheet metal can be easily closed by means of fabric and a rubber solution or "Syndetikon."

REPAIRING DAMAGE TO UNDERCARRIAGE AND SKID.

Damaged undercarriages and skids are difficult to repair, and new parts should be fitted.

The machine can be propped up by means of trestles under the armoured casing.

It should be noted that the trestle under the bottom wing is only for safety against gusts of wind. *Under no circumstances must the weight of the machine be borne by trestles under the wings.*

In cases of extensive damage to the undercarriage a beam should be passed under the fuselage in front, and if necessary behind the bottom wing, and the machine gradually raised by inserting logs under these beams.

SPARE PARTS.

The following spare parts are supplied with every machine :—
- 1 Axle.
- 2 Undercarriage wheels, without tyres.
- 1 Skid with spring.
- 1 Complete set of Interplane struts.
- 2 Turnbuckles to each strut.
- 2 Tubular sockets to each strut.
- 1 Spare propeller.
- 1 Tail skid.
- 2 Trestles for trestling up.
- 1 Lifting jack.
- 1 Case containing repairing material (light sheet metal corrugated and plain, light metal tubes of the required diameter).
- 1 Tool box (hollow riveting apparatus, necessary material for riveting, supply of the most necessary split pins, rivets and screws).

The apparatus for internal riveting can be obtained from the aviation park.

www.ingramcontent.com/pod-product-compliance
Ingram Content Group UK Ltd.
Pitfield, Milton Keynes, MK11 3LW, UK
UKHW051525180426
11947UKWH00019B/1585